"When faith lies flattened by moral
we've lost our shock over the Holy
step to the fore and give us their fi
God, that's exactly what's happening here in these pages.

—**Winn Collier**, author of *Love Big, Be Well* and *A Burning in My
Bones* and director of the Eugene Peterson Center for
Christian Imagination

"This poet–priest serves well both earth and heaven, joining
them to celebrate the voice of the God who speaks into our own
earth–language the echoes of heaven as they arrive to his atten-
tive, listening ear."

—**Luci Shaw**, author of numerous poetry collections including *Reversing
Entropy* and *An Incremental Life* (forthcoming). Writer in
Residence at Regent College, Vancouver, Canada

"Absolutely beautiful. Poems from the heart. I love them!"

—**Anton Lesser**, actor known for his roles in *Game of Thrones*, *Wolf
Hall*, *The Crown*, *Endeavour*, and *Star Wars: Andor*

"This collection has a homiletic core, and I am struck by the hu-
mility, humanity, honesty and humor of these poems. Matthew
White's work continues the beautiful tradition of the Metaphyscial
poets and is especially reminiscent of John Donne and even more
so, George Herbert."

—**Paul Mariani**, poet, author and winner of the John Ciardi Award for
Lifetime Achievement in Poetry as well as the Flannery
O'Connor Lifetime Achievement Award from Loyola
University, Chicago

"These poems will reach straight into your body and squeeze your
heart tight. Thought-provoking and achingly emotive, Matthew
has an honesty and witty grit, no doubt honed at the frontline of
all that is life, which cuts through many layers to land soul-deep."

—**Donna Ashworth**, *Sunday Times* bestselling author and poet

"A deeply raw and moving collection of poems, this is not for readers who want to ignore the twists, turns and depths of humanity, but rather embrace every crevice. Rather than wallowing in the difficulties and mourning that are all part of the human condition, Matt's stirring faith and redirection towards Jesus offers readers hope and solace within the pain. A beautiful and reflective read for deep thinkers and feelers."

—**Lauren Windle**, author of *Notes on Love: Being Single and Dating in a Marriage Obsessed Church*, and *Notes on Feminism: Being a Woman in a Church Led by Men*

"With words as pastoral as they are poetic, gentle as they are stirring, Matthew has, like a true psalmist, written a collection that leaves no stone of the human story unturned. As you move through these pages, you'll find yourself walking the terrain of grief and wonder, beauty and connection, guided by a man who has paid for his words."

—**Joshua Luke Smith**, poet, rapper, producer and founder of The Psalmists

Propelled into Wonder

Propelled into Wonder

Poems of a Priest

Matthew White

ILLUSTRATIONS BY
Sarah White

FOREWORD BY
Simon Ponsonby

RESOURCE *Publications* • Eugene, Oregon

PROPELLED INTO WONDER
Poems of a Priest

Resource Publications
An Imprint of Wipf and Stock Publishers
199 W. 8th Ave., Suite 3
Eugene, OR 97401

www.wipfandstock.com

PAPERBACK ISBN: 979-8-3852-1999-5
HARDCOVER ISBN: 979-8-3852-2000-7
EBOOK ISBN: 979-8-3852-2001-4

VERSION NUMBER 09/11/24

Dedicated to my amazing Dad. Profoundly loved and missed and enjoying the lived reality of his own poetic verse:

Joy

In the end which is no end
Always under the Mercy,
Light-filled and glorious,
I have no need to dream
There, held by Splendor,
No fading of the fascination
And no dulling of the delight—
In the end which is no end

Reverend Canon David White (1958–2021).
Used with permission.

"There is an appointed time for everything. And there is a time for every matter under heaven." —Ecclesiastes 3:1

"Remember His wonders which He has done."
—Psalm 105:5

Contents

Part 3: Tragedies and Comedies

Part 4: Cleaving and Leaving

Part 5: Exploring and Withdrawing

Foreword

MICHAEL LONGLEY, FORMER "Ireland Chair of Poetry," recalls being on a panel of Celtic poets addressing the question, "What is poetry?"[1] They all had a stab at it and then the Welsh bard RS Thomas offered: "*Poetry is the voice of God.*" Longley, who self-described as a "sentimental disbeliever," adds that when they all stopped laughing, Thomas affirmed, "*And so it is.*" RS Thomas was an Anglican priest, and his poetry was inseparable from his Christian faith and ministry in a world infused by God, whether adored or ignored.

The Nigerian Poet, Afam Akeh, is rightly celebrated for his masterful poetry in an article titled, "The poet as priest,"[2] exploring the work of Afam who is both a distinguished poet and a church minister. However, the priestly offering is quizzed by the commentator, Pa Ikhide, who asks whether faith should be brought to poetry and rather tenses at what on occasion he discerns as proselytizing: "*Sometimes his poetry is inspired—and compromised by his near unquestioning allegiance to his Christian faith.*" But the Christian poet cannot hide or be ambiguous or oblique about their faith, for then their poetry would be other than they are, it would become inauthentic, bifurcated, and powerless. The poet is not there to own the worldview of the reader—but to share how they see the world.

In private correspondence with me, Afam brilliantly defined poetry both as "logistics"—"*the fine packaging and measured deployment of aesthetic sensitivity or sensibility to put the best*

1. https://www.irishtimes.com/culture/books/what-is-poetry-three-masters -look-for-answers-1.2255718

2. https://xokigbo.com/2013/09/20/afam-akeh-letter-home-biafran-nights -the-poet-as-priest/

words, sounds and meanings in the best order," but also mystically as "religious aesthetics"—"*God in expression.*" Afam can't have one without the other. And if, as he believes, the earth is the Lord's and the fullness thereof, then poetry that is a window to life on God's earth, even if not self-consciously "religious" will inescapably be spiritual commentary.

And for the Christian poet, the priestly poet, those words take on something of the prophet, for the poet is seer and sayer. Poetry is not simply about rules of rhythm and rhyme, classical literary allusions, alliterations, assonance, contrapuntalism, puns and word plays and all that jazz. Good poetry, like good art, is not painting by numbers. It is about feeling, searching, seeing, trueing. Words are the poet's tools to create something, but they are not that something, for words in poetry work alchemy. Poets place words that sing and dance together, but reach to convey more than words. Many have compared poetry to the sacraments—a sign, a form, a thing that conveys more than the sum and substance of its syntax and sentences.

Certainly the best poetry never leaves you with itself but takes yourself elsewhere. Matthew White's first book of poems (he has previously published worship songs) is titled "*Propelled into Wonder*" and he rightly understands the task and the form. Good poetry stops us and moves us simultaneously. It propels us beyond itself to wonder, and even to woe, and Matt has the heart and the craft of the poet to move us in our soul, his words lead us somewhere, his words precipitate a response.

Matthew White is a priest and a poet, but first a priest. Whilst this is by no means a collection of religious poems, far less proselytizing, it is written in the milieu of faith by a man of faith and it is in service to the eternal Word of God this priestly poet muses. At times amusing and delighting, others disarming and disturbing.

I am not surprised Matt became both priest and a poet. I have known him since he was a teenager busking in the shopping streets of Truro for pocket money on Saturday; then leading in worship the Cornish saints crammed like sardines in his father's church on Sunday. Matt's father, big Dave, was the best friend I ever had, who walked as close to God as any I've known. And he loved life and literature and language and when he spoke of God some said it thundered. My own son each month recalls with joy once standing outside with David on a plenilune, gazing up into the bright-eyed night, when David opened wide his arms, and joyfully bellowed to the seen and unseen, "Look at the moooooooon!" That was poetry. That was being propelled into wonder. Matt is his father's son, and his heavenly Father's son and as priest and poet he invites us to look—to look at ourselves, to look at life, to look at the Church, to look at the Son, and yes, to look at the moon, and be *propelled to wonder.*

Simon Ponsonby is a priest and teacher
based in Oxford, England

Acknowledgments

THIS BOOK WOULD NOT exist without the generosity of many wonderful people. I must start by thanking Sarah, my amazing wife and best friend, who is a modern-day saint! Thank you for your gracious companionship on the journey so far and for lending your skillful illustrations to enhance my feeble words. You are far more beautiful and talented than you realize and it is a dream fulfilled to offer our creative gifts together here.

A huge thank you to my three remarkable children for helping me identify and remedy the full extent of my selfishness! Eli, Ava and Nate, you are all precious gifts of grace and I love you more each day. Thank you for filling my life with your own unique contributions of wonder, joy and audacity. It is a rich blessing indeed to be your Dad. Thank you for being patient with me.

To my ever-loving and ever-proud parents, thank you for everything! Mum, you are inspiration, sage, and rock and I love seeing how the Lord continues to use you to provide encouragement and support to so many. Dad, we all miss you hugely and I would have loved a few more conversations (and pints) with you about ministry, the Anglican Church and the escapades of the England men's cricket team, but your bountiful legacy lives on. We are so incredibly thankful for all the years we spent with you and for everything you blessed us with. Thank you for introducing me to Eugene Peterson, Edward Lear, the Eagles and P.G. Wodehouse.

To Jon and Alex, my beloved brothers, thank you for your friendship and for ensuring that life never becomes overly serious. Our ability to embrace fun, beauty and silliness in equal measure is a rare and life-enhancing gift! Thanks to Anna and Holly also, two fantastic (and civilizing) family additions.

I hold enormous love and affection for a plethora of extraordinary family members and friends (too many to mention here), including all my aunts, uncles, cousins, nieces, nephews and godchildren. A heartfelt and special thanks must also go to the following people: Mac, Barbara, Arthur, Nora, Brian, Liz, Chris, Becky, Trev, Cat, Chris, Kat, Matt, Beks, Gemma, Timo, James, Charlie, Dan, Esther, Alice, Zoë, the Abbeys, the Ponsonbys, and all others who have cheered my tribe and I on over the years. We would not survive without you!

I would also like to thank the various church communities that we have had the privilege of belonging to over the past three decades for all the ways in which you have shaped and encouraged us. We remember you all with great fondness.

I would like to reserve a special thank you for my editor, Matthew Wimer, and the good folk at Wipf & Stock and Resource Publications. I am eternally grateful to you for believing in me and in this project.

A very personal thank you must also go to all those who endorsed the book and to Simon Ponsonby for providing such a generous and poignant foreword and for blessing me so often through his own inspired words and anointed preaching.

Last but by no means least, thank you to Finn and to Emma (the OG) for your loyalty and warmth.

Introduction

I HAVE BEEN WRITING poems for as long as I can remember and there are plenty that do not feature here (for good reason). In the writing and reading of poetry, I have found—and have come to cherish—a mysterious and penetrating means of divine communion which provokes honest expression, awakens the emotions and ignites the imagination. Along the way, it has been impressed upon me that the crafting of poetry demands great care, creativity, playfulness and a keen attention to beauty.

In Psalm 38:9, the psalm's author admits the following: "Lord, all my desire is before You; and my sighing is not hidden from You." This particular collection of poems may be viewed as a conglomeration of various desires and sighs from the past decade which have been brought before the Lord and now before you, the reader. As is so often the case in the lived human experience, these desires and sighs are both light and shadow, godly and ungodly, bringing my perpetual need of redemption into that intoxicating and dynamic waltz of redeeming love.

This poetry collection is not an academic endeavor. It is not primarily concerned with remaining true to certain forms or conventions of poetry. Such a project may materialize in the future. It may not. This collection may not appeal to the purists either, as demonstrated by the condescending response my work received from one such purist (and one of my favorite poets no less!). However, this experience did become the inspiration for a poem in this book. Another tale of redemption.

If nothing else, my hope is that the words on the pages that follow are honest. Moreover, that they are honest in the way that the Psalms are honest, holding nothing back and declining that dangerous invitation to adopt an unrealistic state of permanent politeness, all in the name of showing God due reverence.

As a priest, I revere God and it is precisely because of my reverence *for* God that I am fully honest *with* God. Similarly, as a poet, I revere words. I admire the sounds they make, the meanings they harbor, the possibilities they create and the stories they weave. I am fascinated by both phonology and etymology, and I know that each carefully chosen word will always lead me back to cosmology and to gazing upon the invisible yet ever-so-visible One who "spoke" the world into being.

Over the years, I have come to see that the line between poems and prayers is a blurred one for what are poems if they are not prayers? What is poetry if it is not heartfelt longing, lamenting and envisioning of what *could* be? Our exclamations, machinations, imaginations and protestations are prayers that reach and contend for the beauty which surrounds us—the very same beauty that transcends us—and would encounter us if only we would still ourselves enough to heed its advances.

It is with no small amount of trepidation that I share here—in print for the first time—some of my own mumbled and fumbled attempts at communion with the divine. As you read this book, you will be granted access to moments where my heart has been at its most full as well as its most crushed. And yet, in all of life's joys and cruelties, I have never lost my conviction that life is wonderful. Or to put it another way, that life is full of wonder. As you read these poems, my hope is that you will be propelled into some of that same wonder and intrigue that prompted me to write them in the first place.

— PART 1 —
Breath and Death

"A time to give birth and a time to die . . ."
—Ecclesiastes 3:2

Between The Bays

I love to walk between the bays
where open space dwarfs prior thought
propelling me into wonder,
enticing me into grandeur.

I stare at sea and contemplate
whether God is with me here or
busy orchestrating tides or
neither here nor there or missing.

Fair few benches between the bays—
I have often sat with Susan
as the sun plants salubrious
kisses on my skin, warming hues

to help sense something greater here,
something otherworldly. This peace—
so non-consensually real—
fast becoming tangible home.

Lay me to rest between the bays,
forever to absorb these days.

A Tense Journey

I never thought reading would wound me,
I never thought my dad would die.
But maybe nothing prepares you
for the present tense waving goodbye.

Now when he's thought of or mentioned,
now in the letters and cards,
now in the funeral tributes,
Dad's no longer an "is" but a "was."

This Place

Grace greeted grief in the most unlikely place.
There in the cold clasp of trauma a church
gathered to pay their respects—air their shock—
another life taken immeasurably soon.

It wearies you this mortality so cruel
seeing life snatched when expecting it the least.
Mourners bereft, those shudders in the rain.
How would I feel were it my own child who died?

I glimpsed them both and I held God to account.
Emmanuel, you had better be *with them*!
Suppressing self and remembering my call
I absolved sad sad liquid from my tears.

Tears carry weight far bulkier than words.
Words will never—*never*—bring them back.
Yet I perused shy shelves and dusty pages
hoping to find some suitable locutions.

The news came through on our anniversary.
Hotel break booked—chance of being child–free—
picture us both, desperate for a break from the kids,
picture them both, desperate, breaking for their kid.

Pain so immense that we didn't see them much.
From sheening pillars to supports needing support,
strong marble slabs becoming peeling plaster.
Surely God was in this place but we did not know!

Soon There Will Be Two

Soon there will be two.
Two trophies forged by me and you,
two constructs of genetic glue,
two cocktails of us to view,
soon there will be two.

Soon there will be two.
Two sparks of life to life renew,
two lots of cheek to not subdue,
two stunning smiles to now pursue,
soon there will be two.

Soon there will be two.
Two gifts of grace to guide us through,
two innocents to cling onto,
two miracles of beauty true,
soon there will be two.

Soon there will be two.
Evidence that we withdrew
and in so doing did not withdraw.
Soon there will be two,
maybe someday there'll be more!

Holy Fire

Still these white–hot flames consume
all those vain things that charm me most.

Purging kiln that purifies—
impress your mark on me!

Holy fire that laps my scars—
decant your grace in me!

Cleansing fire to brand and burn—
in furnace am I truly formed.

His Dreams

His dreams
seldom host to fear.

If only
my dreams could mirror his.

I marvel
but fleetingly in kind.

Such endless
wide–eyed fascination,

so restless—
despite eyelids closed tight.

Refreshing
to lack hint of worry.

Nightmares
concepts highly foreign.

Imagine
land of milk and honey.

Ample
intrigue chaperoning,

enthralled,
waking not from wonder.

Sleep now
ponder. Dream his dreams.

Nuance

I rifled through the boxes—
so neat and ordered—trying
to sift through neglect. Dying
to meet that absent stranger.

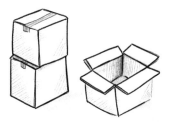

Grandma's Hands

I held those hands one final time
before her light came calling.

So much sunshine in the skinfolds,
so much wisdom in the wrinkles.

So much mischief in the making,
so much courage in the aching.

I held those hands one final time
and listened to the voice of love.

Before her light came calling
I held those hands one final time.

Good Grief

I hate the expression "good grief!"
As if grief could ever be good!
Grief is entirely horrific,
grief is oxymoronic.

Bittersweet,
cruel kindness,
absent presence,
just some (oxy)moronic terms
uttered by (oxy)morons
who, in doubtless well-meaning
but futile endeavor,
attempt to comfort those who mourn.

I vow to resist such utterances!
This is my only choice as my world grows
smaller. My family's sighs are
an open secret and now
we are alone together.

My Father's Pens (Sonnet)

And now my father's pens to me bequeathed!
The ink that flows flaunting such ache in me.
Does inspiration dwell with the bereaved?
Are words the love that cannot come to be?
In gripping I am holding onto him.
In writing I recall the words he wrote.
Why did he die a death so truly grim?
What was the sacred pow'r with which he spoke?
My heart pretends that Dad is here as much
as it is able to blot out the truth.
Whene'er my grief gropes blindly for his touch
I break again and intercede for Ruth.
Confound this crumpled, creased and paper brain!
Now wrong things right with pens to mark the pain.

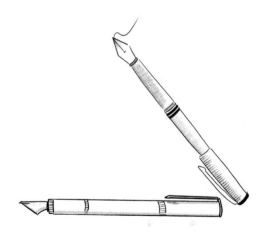

— PART 2 —
Ending and Mending

"A time to kill and a time to heal . . ."
—Ecclesiastes 3:3

Broken

My love I am broken
fractured mess, muddied shards,
limping cripple, guilty
but you and I know now.

My love you are broken
puzzle missing pieces,
shadow of former self
but you and I know now.

My love he was broken
tapestry of scars and
blood—sacrificial pawn—
no longer broken now.

My love we are broken
jagged glass coaxing light.
His strength in our weakness all,
sweet taste of glad defeat.

My love we are broken
beautiful forgeries,
two tainted canvases
but you and I know now.

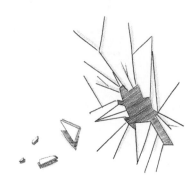

The Spectrum

I am both ends of the spectrum,
a living contradiction.
I am governed by my feelings
and burdened by perfection.

I am both ends of the spectrum,
a toxic conflagration
drinking poison, thinking curses,
rendering myself unfit.

You are both ends of the spectrum,
one end sin, then salvation.
Becoming both friend and brother
unbecoming jilted lover.

Before the spectrum was,
you were.

Mind The Gap

We spend a lifetime widening
and narrowing the gap between.

Public personas, projected misnomers,
playing paying crowds convinced that they know us
all the while loathing ourselves in the shadows.

We spend a lifetime widening
and narrowing the gap between.

Take heed not haste lest feet betray you into
the blackening void your ego created
which puffed–up pride keeps on inflating.

We spend a lifetime widening
and narrowing the gap between.

And for what purpose? What very vanity?
To bury shame and brokenness the further
underground and under skin and underneath.

We spend a lifetime widening
and narrowing the gap between.

Suppressed hearts held by darkening pestilence
until the blackness comes to fruition
and these tethered prisons reach completion.

We spend a lifetime widening
and narrowing the gap between.

Mind the gap.

Three

And now these three remain:
control, despair and cynicism.
But the greatest of these
is cynicism. Sin is schism.

Unfathomable

Grace that roars and reaches for me
in spite of—no, *because* of—those
crimes which I ruled eons ago
rendered me incompatible
with such unfathomable love.

As I condemn and lash myself
for all less–than–worthy living,
unholy thoughts are adopted—
forcibly subverted—fathered
by such unfathomable peace.

You don't correct my wrongs. Rather
you direct my crooked ways to
your oasis of clarity in
arid desert of confused catechisms
and partial doctrines.

Here I can breathe—here I can be—
here warped and waning resistance
yields happy death. O welcome grave!
Willfully dead and blithely free
for this unfathomable Christ

of tender heart and furrowed scars
with bloodied brow and holy crown.
As dumbstruck as I am renewed
by lavished love from high above
and such unfathomable Christ.

Cause And Effect

It's not the rightness or wrongness
nor the validity of cause.

I am not unmoved, not unsympathetic
but I am bored, bored of playing

politics, of straining with eyes
stained by ideology jousts.

Tribalism births inertia.
Factions spew fiction threatening

to expose the true resolve of
my commitment to choose love

and thereby to love regardless.
I hate the hate–tinged so–called

"love" of graceless bigots! And yet
in hating, bigot I become.

Your speck made me an atheist
with great faith in my many planks.

Ruin

Ruin whispers deathly perils
into my futile heart.
Putrid vacuum, pulsing, clinging
mildew darkens belief.

Ocean sorrows plumb their shallows
into my noxious heart.
Shadows flowing. Morose
moments tiptoe closer.

Malaise for days, for days and haze
decays my baneful heart.
Afraid, forlorn, of grace foregone—
praised but never praising.

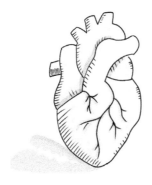

Authenticity

Be yourself.
Be real.
Be honest.

Be fragile.
Be broken.
Be honest.

Be losing.
Be finding.
Be honest.

Be bruised.
Be held.
Be honest.

Be vexed.
Be peaced.
Be honest.

Be swayed.
Be flint.
Be honest.

Be open.
Be hidden.
Be honest.

Be fearless.
Be playful.
Be honest.

Be gentle.
Be frank.
Be honest.

Man cannot build
authentic
community.

Authenticity
lays her own bricks
exposing the

cracks in the
foundations.
Be honest.

Move Toward The Pain

Move toward the pain.
Though shadows render you shy,
drink courage you saints.

Move toward the pain.
Hope fizzes in unfurled hands
waiting to be seized.

Move toward the pain.
Presence is sweet medicine
in this ailing world.

Move toward the pain.
Lay hands on unseen lepers—
the lonely afraid.

Move toward the pain.
Light kisses foragers
groping in the dark.

Move toward the pain.
Let holy scars like ointment
tend to open wounds.

Move toward the pain.
Hear deep calling to deep—
drink courage you saints.

Hope Deferred

The welcome warmed me soliciting
my submission. You scorned me although
rarely has rejection seen me tilt
my ears to each incision of the knife.

— PART 3 —

Tragedies and Comedies

"A time to weep and a time to laugh . . ."
—Ecclesiastes 3:4

Fruitless

The larks have stopped singing comfort.
The wells have given up. Here where

I used to feast on choice morsels
until locusts graffitied ruin.

Where did the life go? Did it leave
when the spited egos arrived?

Pastors have been self–infected
pursuing jargon arousals

manufactured by the nervous
praise of a neglected people.

Mercy used to join us for dinner
to wash the filth from errant sinners.

Long–Forgotten

Holiness—

set apart,
set upon.
Set against,
set in stone.

Set a trap,
set a time.
Set a date,
set a fire.

Set me up,
set me off.
Set a price,
set me free—

sanctity!

The God–Slave

See the God–Slave spit on slavery,
hear him snarl at evil's vagrancy.
See him exploit the exploiters
who've surrendered their humanity.
See the God–Slave.

See the God–Slave weep with righteous rage
as the trafficked have their freedom raped.
When a person's race affects their place
see his arms of grace afford them space.
See the God–Slave.

See the God–Slave on a crucifix,
see him mute the barbarous crack of whips.
See his hands play liberation riffs,
see creation at his fingertips.
See the God–Slave.

See the God–Slave summon you to be
a Wilber–force for setting free,
a Luther–King of equity,
a slave to justice and mercy.
See the God–Slave.

Universe In Reverse

I wish a pterodactyl would land upon my head
and tread my body into the ground.

How different life might be had our remnant fossils
been discovered by the dinosaurs.

Pre-historic visitors would flock to new museums
to gaze on our rebuilt skeletons.

All the bones would be unwieldly—out of order—
curated by some clumsy tyrannosaurs,

their chicken hands so rigid—inflexible digits—
inadvertent new species showcased.

A creature nonetheless but far from conventional
within normal human confines.

A rib cage for a head, feet instead of ears,
legs adorning shoulders like cannons.

Humankind redefined as a tyrannosaurus
wrecks time's witness with withered dexterity.

On second thoughts, bid me rest as fossil lost
to sands of time, in pieces but at peace.

Reflections Upon Marriage

Marriage is beautifully beautiful
when husbands are dutifully dutiful
but wives are irrefutably crazy
when their men are indisputably lazy.

Acrostic Diagnostics (Made Yesterday When I Felt Euphoric)

Skillful
and
resourceful
at
home

serving
and
readying
a
household.

She
always
remedies
aching
hearts

selflessly
accommodating
really
annoying
~~husband~~ housemates.

Scarcely
aware
really
about
how

spellbindingly
astonishing,
redemptive
and
heroic

she
appears.
Refreshing
and
healing

so
ably.
Radiant
angel.
Hope.

Little Children

When Jesus said,
"Let the little children come to me,"[1]
he hadn't met
my progenies when they turned three.

1. Matthew 19:14 (NIV)

I Love Pigs

"I love pigs!"
Three surprising words I did not anticipate
my father pontificating during that December screening of *The Hobbit*.
But the more I ruminated upon his joyous exclamation
the more I noticed a newfound admiration
bubbling within for said muddy mammals.

Today I would urge you to consider that pigs are a picture of peace!
Creatures at ease in their own skin
comfortable with mess, playful
seemingly—almost certainly mischievous—
finding a fulfilled existence in their blissful indifference
to the muck and smells that cling to them.

Pigs are exemplary and inspirational disciples.
Pigs have learned the secret of being content in any and every situation.[2]
Were I as "piggy" as a pig, I'd be far less fickle and far more free,
living as I was knit to be.
Even the ugliness of pigs is endearing.
I envy them.

The grunts of a pig elicit mirth,
the expressions of a pig evoke fond memories
of legendary nights out with friends and disheveled mornings.
Pigs even manage to excel post-mortem since
few things in life can rival bacon.
I love pigs!

2. Philippians 4:12 (NIV)

Limerick

There once was a strange chap from Limerick
who used to converse with a toothpick;
'til one day there came
a Russia–bound plane
whereupon he conversed with a Bolshevik.

Nocturnal Whispers

I tread softly into my children's rooms
ready to decant nocturnal whispers
into whichever exposed ears would
host said sacred impartations.

Children are a blessing—rich gifts from God—
and my quiver is full. Blessed to bless and
now night has come, nocturnal whispers
smuggle truths from my heart to theirs.

My parents ferried nocturnal whispers
to my brothers and I from earliest days
when we were mere knitting projects
each unraveling in the womb.

Strange how we inherit and remember
those liturgies of love uttered over us.
"May the Lord bless and keep you!
May he make his face shine on you!"

(I can still hear my mother singing)

— PART 4 —

Cleaving and Leaving

"A time to embrace and a time to shun embracing . . ."
—Ecclesiastes 3:5

God

I saw God in a vagabond's face.
You could tell that he'd been through a lot.
Eyes vacant seemingly from crying,
ramshackle body, hollow, emptied
and exhumed of everything but love.

For all he had seen and suffered,
no devil or hell could extinguish
that inherent incessant flicker.
Fire within him—refusing to die—
warming even the stiff cold of death.

He told me he had no home because
he resides with the sick and broken,
the lost and the overlooked. He is
often ignored when begging for change.
I heard God in a vagabond's voice.

You could tell that he'd been through a lot.

Legacy

It took his absence to make me see
the lasting impact of his presents

gifted to me, to us all. Full life
of fruit and wonder. Grace upon grace,

eternal inheritance. Gifts fanned
into flames through the laying on of love.

Perpetual portions of divine favor.
Oil cascading from beard to beard,

from father to father, grandfather
to grandchildren, holding the other,

none of it possible without a mother
serving in the shadows fusing,

forging and forming the spotlight saints.
As iron sharpens iron so

one mighty lioness sharpens the others.
No longer here to see it unfold

or cameo in stories untold
yet somehow *still* his proud smile warms me.

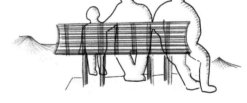

Betrayal

When does deception's infection
undertake its chilling ascent?

Is it that first little look or
that first little white lie?

Could it be that first little sly
harmless misdemeanor?

When did Judas betray Jesus?
When did Jerry betray Robert?

Does betrayal start with plotting
or begin as the plot unfolds?

Is the grass *really* greener there
or just where we choose to water?

Lulworth Cove

I walked the road to Lulworth Cove
upon that cold November morn.
A former charm possessed me there
as my feet dueled with pebbles
themselves like almond jewels beset
upon a golden concave crown.

Did these same waters lap the toes
of bygone champions of prose?
Did Hardy stop and rest awhile
whilst breathing in such beauty
as harkens back to yesteryear
yet illuminates the present?

I muse a life spent by the sea
as I propel more failed skims
into the turquoise shallows. Each
lucid ebb amounting to a
kind of friendly ridicule, a
welcome kind of wistful taunting.

Happy mocked in Lulworth Cove
where whitewashed crags and birds spectate.
Happy lost in Lulworth Cove
where gunfire shall ne'er serenity breach.
Happy loved in Lulworth Cove,
glad spirit given to the sea.

Reluctantly I turn around,
scraping transfixed eyes away from
said nest of witching fascinations
and shuffle up the hilly road
with heavy feet and heavy heart
brimming—mind swimming—with wonder.

Never mine but forever mine,
this cherished unbuilt cathedral.
Never mine but forever mine,
home away from mundane home.
Never mine but forever mine,
beloved Lulworth Cove!

Haiku And I

Immaturity,
the freedom of happiness
found within a friend.

Two lovers fighting
the chorus of the blackbird
beckoning the day.

An unsettled camp,
a dwelling place discovered
nomads far from home.

Smothering mother,
the bounding of a puppy,
newfound family.

Traffic–tainted views
stalling onset of new life,
product of a seed.

Workaholic boss,
two laughing sets of parents
voyaging this life.

Nearly

Offices are cages for the creatively oppressed.
Home is where the soul is and home is where I roam
naked.

I seek reprieves beneath ring-pulls of carbonated drinks
when my cage overdresses me with uninspired rags.
Numb.

Calendars weigh heavy when you are willing them to change.
Time decides to slow so it can tease you in
neuroses.

Sarah lends a purpose to each transitory twist, soon
she will be mine for soon we shall be wed and remade
new.

Days begin to merge and elicit survival instincts
but I am fighting instincts of another kind
nearly.

Imagination

Imagination is the playground of celestial interruption.
Swings squeak and slides may slow yet wonder effervesces.

Without imagination we are but dimly lit,
grabbing at ideas that evade us in the fog.

Eureka moments become tomorrow's masterpieces.
Imagine, create, imagine, create, imagine.

John Lennon urged us to imagine lack of heaven
but life devoid of paradise is life bereft of joy
I imagine.

Prodigal

Look how Father runs
from far desperate
to bear hug Prodigal
pregnant with tears.

It was more than arms
that held Prodigal—
impassioned yearning
of aching parent.

Love held Prodigal
in that moment he
felt weight of welcome
steamrolling his shame.

Celebrated not
castigated! Feast
where flagellation
should have furrowed him.

Invited to be
unquestionably
accepted. Prodigal
could finally breathe!

Grace kissed Prodigal
at last he was home.
Brother's scorn could not
scour smiles from his face.

Cross-Purposes

Red royal sap seeps
down that T–shaped tree
blanketing every
past present future

life—eternal snow
covering those standing
in light of its beams.
Lustrous shadows of

hope. Holy dark shade
shifting shame into
the long grass, coaxing
unbridled soliloquies

from hearts humbled so
by cruciform life
lost no longer and
at a loss for words.

Cross–purposes pierce
stubborn resistance.
Nails pinned Love that day,
held yet ever holding.

Church Inc.

Churches reared by pompous executives are
anathema to grace's paternal nurture!

You can only whitewash tombs for as long as
you can stave off that flood of seeping decay.

There is one Lord, one faith, one baptism[3] and
there were zero NDAs in the Church in Acts.

To neglect prayer is to orphan oxygen,
such arrogance to think we can live without breath!

The kingdom desires mercy not merchandise.
There is only one name to keep exalting.

Mercenaries don't merit platforms that prosper,
egos won't forego the trappings that trip them.

Love with action and with deep sincerity
hate inaction and question scarcity of

hearts aflame with love for God for this is all
there ever was—God of love and love of God!

3. Ephesians 4:5

PART 5

Exploring and Withdrawing

"A time to search and a time to give up . . ."
—Ecclesiastes 3:6

Sunday Boring

Traveling is best when you
look forward to arriving.
If the end-place holds no joy
you hold a wasted ticket.

If residents that greet you
speak patronizing patter
it's no surprise our replies
resemble pre–rehearsed ad–libs.

We judge the people we meet,
we love the people we know,
sing the songs and (try to) walk
weary talk of weathered priests.

Some like walls, some like the halls,
some like the roads outside.
Some like it old, some like new,
others have never questioned.

For all its flaws—and we are them—
there's much here to admire.
The finding of the lost and
the freeing of the bound.

Structures can be useful, this
routine it can be helpful
but be forever watchful
lest these structures stifle you.

Do not neglect the meeting
or care of all those seeking.
I will always love this bride,
this monster, this masterpiece

but—*for God's sake*—don't settle
for a home full of snoring!
Stay in bed, keep snoozing there,
stay clear of Sunday boring!

Failure

Failure is running before walking,
befriending worry before trusting
the hands and plans of God who always
trusted you from the beginning

who unapologetically
pursues your heart and your affections,
stooping low to reassure you in
each and every passing moment.

Heed and do not harden
by holding onto burdens
better left abandoned
to that hurricane of grace.

Failure is crowning yourself early
when your only crowning glory
is your inability to listen
to trauma testimonials that

you ordained cutting corners, weaving
spin to detached directors, blind
and none–the–wiser to your deceit.
Pathetically apathetic.

Heed and do not harden
by holding onto burdens
better left abandoned
to that hurricane of grace.

Failure is shrugging at scars and blood
that tattooed love and would mark you too
if only you'd surrender heart,
if only you'd surrender dark

to each satiating tickle of
salvation's primed and whetted needle.
We never intended to hate you.
You never intended to love us.

Heal and do not harden,
stop hiding in the garden.

The Calling Of Saint Matthew

Puzzled sits the bearded man
in the crosshairs of that finger
which now points to him perhaps
beyond him perhaps before him—
Pointed, nonetheless.

A seemingly sourceless shaft of light
illumines the quizzical gaze
of onlookers looking on the one
who looks their throng with kindly eyes.
Adorned and adored.

Such choice as was is choice as is:
To lay all down and—with unfurled hands—
take hold of grace that takes hold back.
Aren't we all mining for meaning?
Come soon, renaissance!

Waiting Room

Be still and know.

In the waiting room
space is afforded space

    —linger—

no rush, no haste.

Be still and know.

Serve the moment now.
To wait is to slow

    —linger—

I'm saved by grace.

Be still and know.

Keep on waiting,
scream at your striving

    —linger—

and wait to wait.

Be still and know

                     —don't say no to being still—

ears wide open,
noisy silence

                     —linger—

holy truths.

Be still and grow

                     —linger.

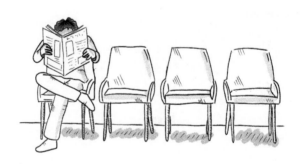

What Matters

What matters is the here and now
not the there and then.

Seize the day! Seize *all* the days!
Create something pure.

Don't dwell on what you had or swell
up on what you want.

Give thanks for what you have received,
this is what matters.

What matters more than family?
What matters more than empathy?

What matters is the way you choose
and how you walk it.

Life is short so pick what matters
lest you filch your joy.

A lock and key, a pharisee,
these do not matter.

The Apostates' Creed

I believe in God who heals.
I believe in God who holds.

I believe in God who was before me.
I believe in God who is after me.

I believe in God who is love.
I believe in God who is pure.

I believe in God who is life.
I believe in God who is light.

I believe in God who died.
I believe in God who thwarted death.

I believe in God who sees.
I believe in God who cares.

I believe in God who listens.
I believe in God who's speaking.

I believe in God who weeps.
I believe in God who grins.

I believe in God who is with me.
I believe in God who is faithful.

I believe in God who is judge.
I believe in God who is grace.

I believe in God who rescues.
I believe in God who redeems.

I believe in God who comforts.
I believe in God who comes close.

But regarding this vocation
with its many expectations

and this broken institution
with its sullied reputation

and my fragile constitution,
I have my doubts.

Penitence

Enter his orbit,
commune with love,
enjoy his delight,
cast thoughts above.

Bask in his goodness,
inhale his life,
bathe in his presence,
imbibe his light.

Seek his forgiveness,
recall your need,
show him the hidden
rest on your knees.

Tarry awhile,
yield to his grace,
treasure his mercy,
yawn at your shame.

Cherish the moment—
be still and know—
collapse into beauty,
behold and glow.

Ponder his whispers,
feast on his word,
paint yourself holy,
fathom his worth.

Humble your ego,
bow to the King,
hallow his name,
bring all to him.

Priestly Manifesto

If, by multiply, you mean
extend the same kindness
extended to you,

If, by strategize, you mean
love intentionally and
with sincerity,

If, by grow, you mean
value depth over
direct debits,

If, by convert, you mean
transform lives with
triune light,

If, by serve, you mean
gladly embrace the
simple small,

If, by build, you mean
demolish ego and
false desires,

If, by succeed, you mean
express—*with courage*—
your purest you,

If, by listen, you mean
turn your ear to the
turned away,

If, by teach, you mean
accept your conduct is
the classroom,

If, by risk, you mean
befriend the beauty of
noble failure,

If, by pioneer, you mean
model hatred of
sin's seduction,

If, by shepherd, you mean
give pasture for
grazed sheep to graze,

If, by nurture, you mean
be a conduit of
divine grace,

If, by befriend, you mean
show kindness that
seeks nothing back,

If, by pray, you mean
show up,
be present,

If, by manage, you mean
survive with
winsome tenderness,

If, by welcome, you mean
purge prejudice and
accommodate all,

If, by stand, you mean
lay down and
prefer the other,

If, by give, you mean
generously deposit your
entrusted blessings,

If, by lead, you mean
cultivate contentment with
secret accomplishments,

Then,
good and faithful servant
you may yet be.

Bed

I clamber into bed and claw for
a device—*any device will do*—
just something to drag me from the dark
and distract me into the distant
possibility of sleep. For here

anticipated anxiety and
racing mind may finally succumb
to that elusive utopia
of unlikely slumber, slippery
as it evades my eyes once more.

Marine Meditations

Vociferous crashing of waves
akin to amplified blessings
serenading the day's fresh hope
ushered in by juvenile swells.

Dehydrated sand quenched by
encroaching liquid—saline salve—
covering all like the divine grace
relentlessly enfolding us.

Such ebbs and flows may not be mastered,
obscured depths may bid us play.
Frolic freely, choose wisely, soon
tides will pull us further on or under.